A Parent Council® Selection

What on Earth Do You Do When Someone Dies?

by Trevor Romain

Edited by Elizabeth Verdick

free spirit
PUBLISHING®

Helping kids
help themselves™
since 1983

Library of Congress Cataloging-in-Publication Data
Romain, Trevor.
    What on earth do you do when someone dies? / by Trevor Romain ; edited by Elizabeth Verdick.
        p.   cm.
    Includes bibliographical references.
    Summary: Describes the overwhelming emotions involved in dealing with the death of a loved one and discusses how to cope with such a situation.
    ISBN 1-57542-055-4
    1. Grief in children—Juvenile literature.   2. Bereavement in children—Juvenile literature.   3. Adjustment (Psychology) in children—Juvenile literature.   [1. Death.   2. Grief.]
I. Verdick, Elizabeth.   II. Title.
BF723.G75R65   1999
155.9'37—dc21

                                                                98-47611
                                                                CIP
                                                                AC

15 14 13 12 11 10 9
Printed in Canada

Free Spirit Publishing Inc.
217 Fifth Avenue North, Suite 200
Minneapolis, MN 55401-1299
(612) 338-2068
help4kids@freespirit.com
www.freespirit.com

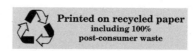

I would like to thank the following experts who read my book and helped me understand how children cope with grief:

William C. Kroen, Ph.D., LMHC

Thomas S. Greenspon, Ph.D.,
Licensed Psychologist

Harry Rauch, M.D.,
Child and Adolescent Psychiatrist

Debi Sharp, LSW

I greatly appreciated your
helpful comments and feedback.

Contents

Introduction

In November of 1997 my dad, Jac Romain, died. I was so shocked that all I could say was . . . *wow*. I couldn't sleep. My stomach hurt, and I didn't want to eat. The whole world seemed different to me. When someone you love dies, it's normal to feel shocked, sad, confused, worried, scared, or a lot of other painful feelings.

I decided to write this book in honor of my dad, who taught me to write and draw and care about other people. After his death, writing helped me sort out my feelings and remember all of the ways my dad was special. It gave me a way to feel more peaceful inside.

I also wrote this book to honor the kids I work with at the Brackenridge Hospital in my hometown. They have cancer, and I visit the hospital to talk with them and make them laugh. Over the years, some of the kids I've made friends with have lost their battle against cancer. Although I was very saddened by their deaths, I can't help but smile when I think about all the good times we had.

Most of all, I wrote this book for you. If you've lost a loved one or someone you cared about, I hope my book answers the questions you have. I hope it gives you the words and strength you need during this painful time in your life. And I hope you believe me when I say that you won't always feel as sad and hurt and confused as you do now. Maybe not right away, but in the coming weeks or months, *you will feel better.*

Trevor Romain

Why do people have to die?

When we're born, we experience life. When our life ends, we experience death. Death happens to all living things on earth.

Some people die when they're really old. Others die when they get very, very sick with an illness like cancer or heart disease. Still others die from being badly hurt in an accident. No matter how someone dies, family and friends of that person feel sad and upset.

My 14-year-old friend Vicki, who had cancer, was very wise for her age. One time, we were talking about dying, and she told me something important. She said that people don't talk about death very often, which makes it harder to understand. And when you don't understand something, you're more likely to be afraid of it. Instead of being scared, talk to someone you love about what's on your mind.

Am I going to die, too?

If someone close to you has died, you may be afraid that you're going to die. It may help to know that most people live for a long, long time, and you probably will, too.

You may also wonder if other people you love or care about are going to die. It's natural to worry like this. In fact, these kinds of fears can keep you awake all night.

It's like worrying about a monster in your closet. It can be scarier to lie in bed alone thinking about the monster than to open the closet and see what's really there. The best way to deal with something you're afraid of is to face it. How? Talk about it. Let somebody know that you feel frightened.

Who can I talk to?

The adults in your life may be so upset about the death that they forget to talk to you about how you're doing. But the more you discuss the death, the less scary it becomes. If you're wondering who you can talk to, here are some ideas:

- your mom, dad, or another family member

- a neighbor or friend of the family

- someone at your place of worship

- your teacher or principal

- a counselor or youth group leader

This is what you can say:

- "I'm scared and confused. What can I do?"

- "I really miss him."

- "I'm sad that I can't talk to her anymore."

- "I'm so lonely, I need some extra love."

- "I need a hug."

What is it like to die?

No one alive knows exactly what it's like to die. When people die, life leaves their body. They can't think, move, feel, or breathe. They can't tell anyone else what death is like.

You might have heard stories about people who almost died. Some of them believe they saw things (like a bright light) or heard things (like the voices of people who died before them). But no one knows for sure if these stories are true.

I like to believe that death is calm and peaceful. I was with my young friend René when she died, and I saw her smile right before she passed away. I'll never forget her peaceful smile.

Why am I hurting so much?

When someone you love dies, your feelings get all stirred up. You may be full of tears, anger, worry, and hurt. You might feel so sad and upset that you want to curl up in a ball and hide. This is because you're experiencing grief. Grief is the deepest sadness a person can feel.

It helps to be able to name and describe all of your feelings. Ask yourself how you feel right now. Are you:

Sad?

Angry?

Shocked?

Scared?

Lonely?

Confused?

Hurt?

Numb
(you don't feel anything)?

Helpless?

Stressed out?

**Disbelieving
(you can't believe the
person really died)?**

Nervous?

Upset?

Worried?

(If none of these words fit your feelings, think of some words that do. You can write the words and draw how you feel.)

When you're hurting deeply inside, you may not feel like eating. You may have bad dreams or trouble sleeping at night. You may even find yourself searching for the person who died (though you know he or she isn't coming back). And you may be hoping, wishing, and praying to see the person again.

Your mind and body are working very hard to deal with what has happened.

Is it okay to cry?

Sometimes people who have lost a loved one pretend like the death didn't happen. Or they act like they aren't hurting as much as they really are. Either way, they keep their feelings locked inside.

If you're keeping your feelings locked up, it's like building a huge wall around yourself—a wall that no one can climb over. What can you do to break down this wall? You can cry.

Crying is okay. You don't have to hide your feelings or put on a brave face. No matter what anyone might say, you aren't a baby or wimp if you cry. Crying helps you set your feelings free.

Is the death my fault?

One question many kids ask is "Was it my fault the person died?" They wonder "Was it because I was bad or didn't say my prayers?" Or "Could I have done something to stop the death from happening?"

If you're having these thoughts, you're feeling guilty. You're blaming yourself for the death (but you shouldn't). Here's something you need to understand: *If someone you love dies, it's not your fault.*

Sometimes, when kids know that someone is dying or has died, they have a dream about the person. In the dream, they may see the person die, and they believe it's *their* fault it happened. Have you had this kind of dream? If you have, you need to know that your dream didn't cause the death.

26

This is really important, so I'll say it one more time: *If someone you love dies, it's NOT your fault.*

What if I just want to be left alone?

After my dad died, there was a brief time when I wanted to be left alone. I didn't know what to feel, say, or do. I trembled a lot and walked around in a daze. It was like a bad dream.

I didn't want anyone to hug me or hold me. People wanted to comfort me, but I pushed them away. You might feel like this yourself. Maybe you don't want people to know how sad you are. Or maybe you're too upset to talk.

Part of you may wish everyone would just go away. But another part of you, deep down inside, probably needs people more than ever. Let your family and friends help you. You can help them, too.

Sometimes it's fine to be alone. You may want to sit and think about the person who died. Just make sure you don't spend *too* much time by yourself.

What can I do if I'm angry?

Some kids feel angry after the death of a loved one. They say "This is so unfair!" Or "Why did this have to happen to me!?" They're mad about what they've lost, and missing the person makes them even madder.

If you feel this way, you might yell at people you love or say things to hurt them. You might take things out on your friends or your pet, even though you don't mean to.

Instead, you can learn to take care of your anger. When you get mad, you can:

- talk to someone about your feelings

- hit your bed with your fists

- go to a field or park and yell

- run, throw a ball, or swim

- take your dog for a long walk

- pound and squash a piece of clay as hard as you want

Will I ever feel better?

Feelings like sadness, anger, and worry will probably hit you in waves. One moment, you'll feel better. And the next, you'll feel worse than ever. You may go up and down like a roller coaster.

Maybe you're wishing for a magic formula to take away the pain you're feeling. Unfortunately, there isn't one, but on the next page there are three good things you can do to help yourself.

#1 *Stay active.* Go outdoors, run around, and shout out loud.

#2 *Show your feelings.* Cry, if you need to, and talk to your family or friends. When you hurt a lot, be sure to get a hug from someone you love. Or give your pet a hug.

#3 *Keep a journal about your feelings.* A journal is a book for writing and drawing your private thoughts.

If you like the idea of keeping a journal, get a blank book or notebook. Or use a sketchbook. This will be your special place to write or draw how you feel.

Use this journal for as long as you need to. Work on it alone or with others. You can share your art and writing, if you want. Or you can keep it to yourself.

Is it still okay to have fun?

Here's something my 7-year-old friend Audrey told me before she died: "Having fun is a good way to forget about things that make you sad." Even though someone you love has died, you can still smile and laugh and enjoy life. It may help to keep a list of things that make you smile—a Smile List! You can look at it whenever you need cheering up.

Most people agree that the person who died would *want* you to go on with your life. Stay busy and spend time doing the things you normally do, like playing and talking to your friends. This is a good way to make the hurt not hurt so much.

Where has the person gone?

One of the hardest things to understand is what happens after people die. Where do they go? Are they in heaven with God? Are they spirits or ghosts?

Different people have different beliefs about what happens after death. Christians, Jews, and Muslims believe that the dead come to life again with God (though their names for God differ). Hindus and Buddhists see death as a cycle in which people die and are reborn in another form. If you're not sure what to believe, talk to your parents about your family's religious faith or beliefs.

What happens to the person's body?

People all over the world take care of their dead in different ways. In many cultures, washing and dressing the person who died is very important. After the body has been prepared in a special way, it may be placed in a coffin or casket. These are chests to bury someone in.

Many kids are curious about what a dead body looks like. They wonder if it will be scary or gross. After the body is prepared, the person who died usually looks calm and at peace. The eyes and mouth will be closed, as if the person were asleep.

Another method of taking care of the body is a process called cremation. This means the body is burned in very high heat. After cremation, only ashes remain.

Being burned or buried may sound terrible, but the person who died can't feel these things when they happen.

If the person who died is cremated, the family might keep the ashes at home in a special vase known as an urn. Some families bury the ashes in the ground. Other families scatter the ashes in a place that was loved by the person who passed away.

For example, my friend Howard loved a mountain close to where he lived. When he died, his parents went to the top of the mountain and scattered Howard's ashes into the wind.

The next spring, pretty flowers bloomed along the mountainside. Howard's parents said that his colorful spirit was captured in each and every flower.

How do we honor
the person who died?

Different families have special ways to honor someone who has died. They may wear certain colors like black or white as a sign of respect. Some families pray, some dance, some light candles, and some hold a feast. Others cover all the paintings and mirrors in their house. And still others burn incense or paper goods. These traditions have been passed down in families for years and years.

Some families hold a ceremony known as a wake or viewing. This is where families "watch over" the dead, or look at the person one last time. The idea of a wake can be confusing. It doesn't mean the person is "awake" or will "wake up." If you don't feel comfortable seeing the body, talk to an adult you trust.

What is a funeral or memorial service?

Some families hold a ceremony called a funeral. This type of service often takes place in a house of worship or a building called a funeral home. Another kind of ceremony is a memorial service, which may be held in a house of worship or in some other place that was special to the person who died.

At these services, family and friends talk about their loved one, sing, pray, or play music. This is how they mourn the loss of the person, or express their grief.

Funerals, memorial services, and other ceremonies like this are important. But your parents may not want you to go. They may think you'll be too sad or frightened.

If you want to go to the service, ask your parents or other relatives. But if you aren't allowed to go, you can still mourn your loved one in your own special way. You can:

• make a hand-drawn card

• think about the person who died

- write your favorite memory or a story about him or her

- gather things the person gave you (like letters or gifts) and spend time looking at and touching them

- say out loud "I love you and miss you"

Your parents and other relatives will be sad on the day of the funeral or memorial service. Sometimes it's hard for kids to see adults cry. Remember that crying sets feelings free—for anyone, no matter what age.

(My 6-year-old friend Alex told me that the best thing you can do for someone who is really sad is hold their hand.)

The service may make you feel like crying and smiling at the same time. You may miss the person who died, but you may also think about the good times you had together. Whether you feel sad or comforted (or both), you can show it by giving hugs or holding hands with other people who are there.

After the ceremony, the person who died may be taken away in a hearse. This special car is usually black or dark gray.

Family and friends may follow behind in their cars as the hearse drives to the cemetery, the place where the body is laid to rest.

Here the coffin or casket is placed in a grave, which is a hole in the ground. The grave may later be marked with a special memorial called a headstone.

Some headstones are big and fancy. Others are simple markers set flat into the ground.

If you've seen a cemetery in a scary movie, you may think it's an awful place to go. Many movies show frightening cemeteries that are dark and filled with ghosts. Actually, most cemeteries *aren't* scary. They're quiet and peaceful.

You won't see ghosts, but you will see graves, headstones, and lots of flowers. Loved ones bring flowers to honor their dead.

How can I say good-bye?

There are many ways to say good-bye to someone who dies. You can visit the grave and say good-bye out loud. Or you can just say it softly to yourself. You can write a good-bye letter or draw a good-bye picture. Do whatever helps you feel better and more peaceful inside.

I said good-bye to my dad by sitting by myself in his art studio and talking to him as if he were there. I told him that I would look after my mom, and my brother and sister. I let him know that I'd never forget him.

I remember my dad each day by keeping a photo of him on my desk in my writing studio. When I look at his picture, I think of the happy times I had with him. Sometimes I just look at him and cry a little. Either way, I feel better.

Here are some ways to remember someone who has died:

- Put photos of the person in a special album.

- Plant a tree or
flower garden
in memory of
the person.

- Have a get-together with family and friends, so all of you can remember the good times.

- Ask your family to light
a candle every year on
the person's birthday.

- Tell your friends how special the person was to you.

- Dedicate a basketball, soccer, baseball, or other game in honor of the person.

- Give money (in the name of the person who died) to a special organization. You may want to ask your parents for help with this idea.

- Visit the place where the person is buried.

- Draw a picture of your loved one or write a poem in his or her honor. You can display it in your room, or place it on the grave or by the urn where the ashes are kept.

- Put something belonging to your loved one in a secret place that only you know about. Look at it when you're feeling sad or just want to remember.

What happens to me now?

When someone you love
dies, your life is different
than before. If you've
lost a parent, you may
wonder who will take
care of you now. If you've
lost a brother, sister, or
close friend, your life may
feel emptier.

These kinds of changes are hard to accept. If
you're worried about your future, talk to an adult
who will understand. Ask this person for advice
(and a hug, if you need one).

It also helps to talk to your friends. They may be afraid to call you or invite you over because they know you're feeling sad. You can let them know that you still want to be friends. Tell them it's okay for them to talk to you about the death, and even ask you questions. Remind your friends that they don't have to treat you differently.

As time goes by, you'll begin to feel less worried, sad, angry, confused, and lonely. It may not seem possible, but it's true. Time helps heal the pain.

On birthdays, holidays, and other special days, memories of the person who died may come flooding back. You may be sad all over again. If you're grieving during these times, share your thoughts and memories. Let the people who love you know how you're feeling.

You may have lost someone special to you, but something will always remain—your memories. Hold tight to these memories by looking at your photos, keepsakes, drawings, or journal. Think about how much the person meant to you, and about all the fun times you shared. You may find it comforting to remember your loved one's smile, voice, or laugh.

There's one more very important thing you need to know: *Remembering* can help someone live on forever . . . in your mind and in your heart.

Where else can I go for help?

You can find more information about coping with the death of a loved one and dealing with your grief. Ask a parent or other adult to take you to a local library or bookstore. Your school library can be a good resource, too.

The Dead Bird by Margaret Wise Brown, illustrated by Remy Charlip (New York: Harper Trophy, 1995). Originally published in 1958, this book tells the story of some children who find a dead bird, bury it, and say their good-byes. For ages 4–8.

The Fall of Freddie the Leaf by Leo F. Buscaglia (Austin, TX: Holt, Rinehart & Winston, 1983). This story explains life and death in terms of the passing seasons. For ages 9–12.

The Tenth Good Thing About Barney by Judith Viorst, illustrated by Erik Blegvad (New York: Atheneum, 1971). When Barney the cat dies, his young owner feels so sad that he can't do anything. His mother suggests that he write a list of ten good things about Barney, so the boy can think about all the good times they had. For ages 4–8.

When Dinosaurs Die: A Guide to Understanding Death by Laurie Krasny Brown and Marc Brown (Boston: Little, Brown and Company, 1996). The words and pictures in this helpful book explain death, grief, and how to cope. For ages 4–8.

About the author/illustrator

When South African-born Trevor Romain was 12, his teacher told him he wasn't talented enough to do art, but 20 years later he discovered that he could draw. He has since written and illustrated 30 children's books, and he has an animated video series for kids based on his best-selling, award-winning books. Trevor also visits schools to speak to children, and he spends his free time with kids who have cancer at the Brackenridge Hospital in Austin, Texas.

To place an order or to request a free catalog of SELF-HELP FOR KIDS® and SELF-HELP FOR TEENS® materials, please write, call, email, or visit our Web site:

Free Spirit Publishing Inc.
217 Fifth Avenue North • Suite 200 • Minneapolis, MN 55401-1299
toll-free 800.735.7323 • local 612.338.2068 • fax 612.337.5050
help4kids@freespirit.com • www.freespirit.com